SACRED MUSIC
Made Easy To Play

SACRED MUSIC MADE EASY TO PLAY

Arranged By
ARTHUR BAYAS

-CONTENTS-

Cover & Design
JOHN OCCHUITO

AMAZING GRACE

Moderately
F#-B-D
A - maz - ing grace! How sweet the
sound that saved a wretch like me!
I once was lost, but now am
found, Was blind but now I see.

2. 'Twas grace that taught my heart to fear,
   And grace my fears relieved.
   How precious did that grace appear,
   The hour I first believed!

3. Yes, when this heart and flesh shall fail,
   And mortal life shall cease,
   I shall possess within the veil,
   A life of lasting peace.

I WALKED INTO THE GARDEN

Text: Dale White

Music by
Marion Weaver

Slowly
mf I walked in-to the gar-den they
call Geth-se-me-ne, And there it was I
knew the Sa-viour died for me. I
walked in-to the gar-den and breathed the pur-est
air, It was a love-ly gar-den for Je-sus had been there.

PANIS ANGELICUS
(Bread of Angels)

Slowly
Music: Cesar Franck
p O bread of an - gels, Food__ for the starv - ing soul, O bread ce - les - tial,__ O Lord, we plead for this dole. Send thru Thy glo - rious might, In dark - ness and in light, Pa - nis An - gel - i - cus, bread of life!

SOFTLY AND TENDERLY

Moderately
William L. Thompson
Soft - ly and ten - der - ly, Je - sus is
call - ing, Call-ing for you and for me.
See, on the por - tals He's wait - ing and watch-ing,
Watch-ing for you and for me.

CHORUS

D
G
mp Come home, ___ Come home, ___
A7
D
A
D
Ye who are wear-y, come home. ___
G
C
G
Earn-est-ly, ten-der-ly, Je-sus is call-ing,
C
G
D7
G
Call-ing, O sin-ner, come home. ___

I LOVE TO TELL THE STORY

Words: Katherine Hankey

Music by
William Fischer

Moderately
mf
I love to tell the sto - ry of
un - seen things __ a - bove, Of Je - sus and His
glo - ry, Of __ Je - sus and His __ love. I
love to tell the sto - ry, Be-cause I know 'tis __

D   C   G
true.   It   sat - is - fies my   long - ings,   As
C   G   CHORUS: D
noth - ing else can   do.   f I   love   to tell the
G   C   G
sto - ry!   'Twill   be   my theme in   glo - ry,   To
C   G   D7   G
tell   the   old — old   sto - ry   Of   Je - sus and His love

HOLD THOU MY HAND

Moderately slow
Clarence S. Briggs
The night comes on, My wea-ry eyelids close, The
time draws near when I must seek re - pose. I
kneel to Thee, O Fa-ther of us all, I pray that
Thou will hear my plead - ing call.
Same tempo
Hold Thou my hand, dear Lord, Hold

C7
A7
Dm
Thou my hand. I do not
C°
Am E Am C7
ask to see nor un - der - stand.
F
C7
E7 E
On - ly that Thou will be con - stant - ly
Am
C7
F E
F
Db7
near to me, Hold-ing my hand, dear Lord,
F
C7
F
Hold - ing my hand.

THE NAVY HYMN
(Eternal Father. Strong To Save)

Text: Rev. William Whiting

Music by
Rev. John B. Dykes

Slowly
mf E- ter - nal Fa -ther, strong to save, Whose
arm hath bound the rest - less wave, Who bids the might - y
o - cean deep, Its own ap - point - ed
lim - its keep. Oh hear us when we cry to Thee, For
those in per - il on the sea! A - men.

IN GOD WE TRUST

Music by
Richard Wagner

Slowly

mf In God we trust, Know-ing He stands here be-side us. In God we trust, Know-ing His love will ev-er guide us — Thru the dark of the night, In - to days clear and bright. We must fol-low the right and the just____ if in God we trust. A - men.

* Anglicized from "In Gott Liegt Unser Sehle", a German hymn
based on theme in Wagner's "Tannhauser")

JESU, JOY OF MAN'S DESIRING

Music by
Johann Sebastian Bach
Slowly
C
C7
F   Bb   C   Bb   F   C
Je - su,   joy   of   man's de -   sir - ing,
Thou whose   wis - dom   so   in -   spir - ing
F   Bb   F   Bb   F   C7   F
Thou whose   love tran - scends ev - 'ry mor - tal   fear.
Guides us   thru   the   days   of   an earth - ly   year,
C7   D7   Gm   Am   D7   Gm   Cm
Son   of   God,   we   kneel   be - fore Thee,

* Pronounced "Hay-soo"

Gm F Bb Cm F7 Gm Bb F Bb
Hum - bly now do we im - plore Thee, Guide us
F Dm Gm F C
to the truth un - known,
* (Instrumental solo)
C7 F Bb F Dm Gm F C7
Guide us from Thy heav - en - ly
F C7 F C7 F
throne. Guide_ us from_ Thy heav - en - ly throne.
f

JUST A CLOSER WALK WITH THEE

Verse
Slowly
C   E7 Am   C C° G7
p 1. I   am weak but Thou art strong,____
Dm6 G7   C   Dm G
Je - sus, keep me from all wrong.____
C7   F   Ab C°
I'll be sat - is - fied as long____   As I
C   G7   C
walk, let me walk close to Thee.____

CHORUS
C E7 Am C C° G7
mf Just a clos - er walk with Thee,____
Dm6 G7 C Dm G
Je - sus, grant my hum-ble plea!____
C7 F Fm C°
Dai - ly walk-ing close to Thee,____ Let it
C G7 C
be, dear Lord, let it be.____

2nd Verse:

Through this world of toil and snares,
If I falter, Lord, who cares?
Who with me my burden shares?
None but Thee, oh dear Lord, none but Thee.

(Repeat CHORUS)

SEND THE LIGHT

With spirit
Charles H. Gabriel
mf There's a call comes ring-ing o'er the
rest-less wave, "Send the light! Send the light!"There are
souls to save, "Send the light! Send the
light!" Send the light!_ the bless-ed
gos-pel light, Let it
shine_ from shore to shore! Send the light!_ the bless-ed
gos-pel light, Let it shine_ for-ev-er-more.

NEARER, MY GOD, TO THEE

Moderately
Lowell Mason
Near - er, my God, to Thee, Near-er to Thee
E'en though it be a cross that rais - eth me,
Still all my song shall be: Near-er, my God, to Thee,
Near - er, my God, to Thee, Near - er to Thee!

MY FAITH LOOKS UP TO THEE

Lowell Mason
Moderately
mf
My faith looks up to Thee, Thou lamb of
Cal - va - ry, Sav - iour di - vine. Now hear me
while I pray, Take all my guilt a - way, O let me
from this day be whol - ly Thine! A - men.

ROCK OF AGES

Text by
A.M. Toplady
Music by
Thomas Hastings
Moderately
C   F   C
mf
Rock of A - ges, cleft for me, Let me
G7   C   G7
hide my-self in Thee. Let the wa - ter and the
C   G7   C
blood, From Thy wound - ed side which flowed, Be of
G7   C
sin the dou-ble cure, Save from wrath and make me pure.

LEAD KINDLY LIGHT

Text by
J. H. Newman

Music by
J. B. Dykes

Slowly
Lead, Kind-ly Light, a - mid the en-cir-cling gloom,— Lead Thou me on. The night is
dark and I am far from home,— Lead Thou me
on.— Keep Thou my feet, I do not ask— to—

G   C   G   D7 G
see The dis-tant scene, One step e-nough__ for me.

JESUS, THE VERY THOUGHT OF THEE

Text
Bernard of Clairvaux

Music
J. B. Dykes

Moderately
G   D7   G Am   D7   G
Je-sus, the ver-y thought of Thee,
p

A   D   C D7 E   Am   A
With sweet-ness fills the breast, But sweet-er far Thy
mf

D   G C G   D7   G
face to see, And in Thy pres-ence rest.

O HAPPY DAY

Text by
Philip Doddridge

Music by
E.F. Rimbault

Brightly
O hap-py day, that fixed my choice
O hap-py day, how I re- joice,
On Thee, my Sav - iour and my God,
Be-cause of Thee, the Son of God.
Hap - py day, Hap - py day,
When Je - sus washed my sins a - way!

G
C   G
He taught me how   to watch and   pray,
C   G
4   5   4   2
1
And live re - joic - ing ev - 'ry   day.
G   D   G   D   G   D   G
O   hap - py   day,   O   hap - py   day,
p
C   G   D7   G   D7   G
When Je - sus   washed   my sins a - way!

KUM BA YAH
(Come By Here)

Slowly
Kum ba yah, my Lord,
Come by here, my Lord,
Kum ba yah!
Come by here!
Kum ba yah, my Lord,
Let me hear your voice
Kum ba yah!
Come by here!
Kum ba yah, my Lord,
Help me find my way,
Kum ba yah!
Come by here!
Oh Lord,
Oh Lord,
Kum ba yah!
Come by here!

ABIDE WITH ME

Text by
Henry Lyte

Music by
William Monk

Slowly
A - bide with me, fast falls the e - ven -
tide. The dark - ness deep - ens, Lord, with me a -
bide. When oth - er help - ers fail and com - forts flee
Help of the help - less, O a - bide with me.

FAITH OF OUR FATHERS

Text by
Frederic Faber

Music by
Henri Hemy

Moderately
Faith of our fa - thers, liv - ing still,
In spite of dun - geon, fire __ and sword,
Oh how our hearts __ beat high with joy,
When -e'er we hear that glo - ri - ous word!

Bb   F   C   F
Faith of our fa - thers, ho - ly faith!
f
C7 F   Bb   C7   F
We will be true to Thee 'til death.
p

HEAR A PRAYER, O LORD

Calmly

George Whelpton

D   A   D
Hear a prayer, O Lord, Hear a prayer, O Lord, In-
mp
D7 G   D A7   D   G D
cline Thine ear to us, And grant us Thy peace. A-men.

JESUS, LOVER OF MY SOUL

Text by
Charles Wesley

Music by
Simon Marsh

Allegro
F
C7
F
Bb
F
C7
F
F
Bb
F
Bb
F
C7
mf
1. Je - sus, lov - er of my soul,
2. While the rest - less wa - ters roll,
Let me to Thy bos - om fly,
While the tem - pest still is high,
Hide me, O my Sav - iour, Hide 'til the storm of
life is past, Safe in - to the ha - ven

F
Bb
F
C7
F
guide, O re - ceive my soul at last.

JESUS CALLS US

Text by
Cecil Alexander

Music by
William Jude

With spirit
G
D7
G
Je - sus calls us, O'er the tu - mult of our
mf
C
B
E7
A
D7
life's wild, rest - less sea. Day by day, His sweet voice
G
G7
C
D7
G
sound - eth, Say-ing "Christ-ian, fol - low me."

SWEET HOUR OF PRAYER

Text by
William Welford

Music by
William Bradbury

Moderately

Sweet hour of pray'r! Sweet hour of pray'r, That
calls me from a world of care, And bids me at my
Fa-ther's throne, Make all my wants and wish-es known. In
sea - sons of dis - tress and grief, My soul has of-ten

ARMY HYMN
(Taps)

C   G7   C
found re-lief, And oft es-caped the
F   C   G7   C
tempt-er's snare, By thy re-turn, Sweet hour of pray'r.
Very slow
TROMPET UP 1 OCTAVE
G
Day is done, gone the sun, From the lake and the hill and the
p
D7   G
sky. All is well, safe-ly rest, God is nigh.

ONWARD, CHRISTIAN SOLDIERS

Text by
S. Baring-Gould

Music by
Arthur Sullivan

On-ward, Chris-tian sol - diers,
March-ing, as to war,
With the cross of
Je - sus, Go - ing on be - fore.
Christ, the roy-al
Mas - ter,
Leads a - gainst the foe.

Gm F Bb F C7 F Bb F C7 F
For-ward in - to bat - tle,__ See His ban-ners
Refrain:
C F Gm
go. On-ward, Chris-tian sol - - diers,__
C7 F
March-ing, as to__ war, With the cross of
Bb F C7 F
Je - sus, Go-ing on be - fore.

THE SON OF GOD GOES FORTH TO WAR

Text by
Robert Heber

Music by
Henry Cutler

Moderately
The Son of God goes forth to war, A King-ly crown to gain. His blood red ban-ner streams a-far, Who fol-lows in His train? Who best can drink His cup of woe, Tri-um-phant o-ver pain? Oh

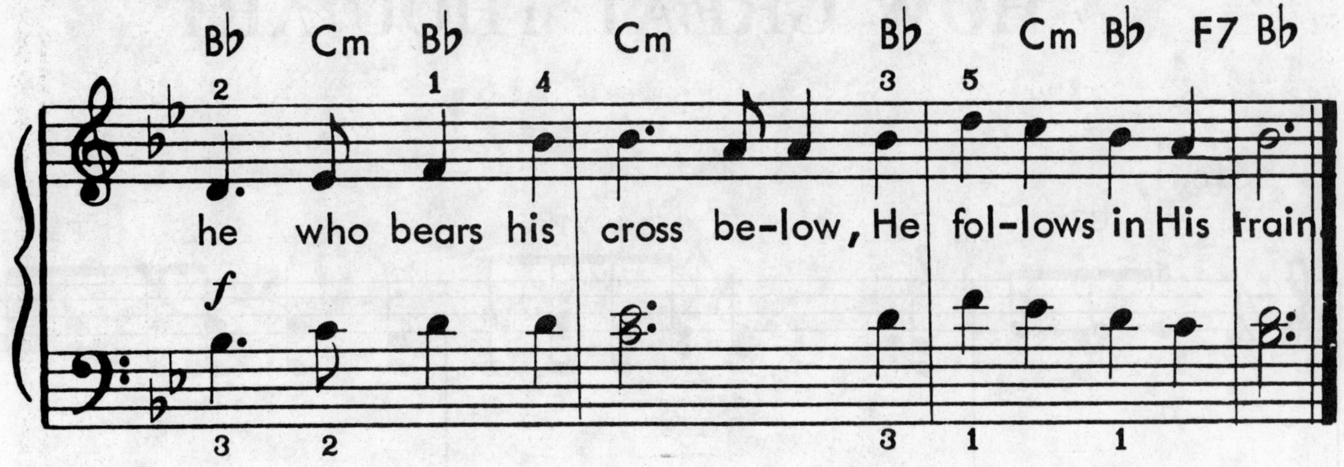
Bb Cm Bb Cm Bb Cm Bb F7 Bb
he who bears his cross be-low, He fol-lows in His train
f

NOW THE DAY IS OVER

Slowly

Joseph Barnby

G D7 G
1. Now the day is o - ver,
2. Now my thoughts are turn - ing
p
C B Am C A7
Night is draw - ing __ nigh, ____ Shad - ows of the
Un - to Thee, dear __ Lord. ____ In my heart O
D7 G D G
eve - ning Steal a-cross the sky.
Je - sus, Thoughts of Thee are stored.

HOW GREAT THOU ART

Gm F F° F
C
G7 F C
Gm F F° F
C Dm G7 C
cresc.
rit.
p
Dm
C
dim.

FAIREST LORD JESUS

With movement
mf   Fair - est Lord   Je - sus!   Rul - er of all
na - ture!   O Thou of God and___ man the
Son!   Thee will I cher - ish, Thee will I
hon - or, Thou   my soul's glo-ry,   joy and crown!

HOLY, HOLY, HOLY

Text: Robert Heber

Music:
John B. Dykes

Moderately with dignity

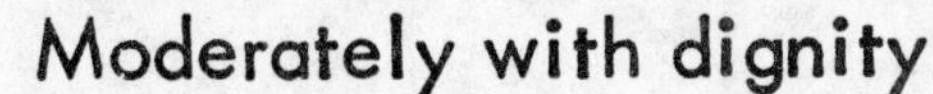

Ho - ly, Ho - ly, Ho - ly! Lord God Al-
might - y! Ear - ly in the morn - ing our
song shall rise to Thee. Ho - ly, Ho - ly,
Ho - ly! Mer-ci-ful and might -y! God in Three
Per - sons, Bless - ed Trin - i - ty.

COME, THOU ALMIGHTY KING

Slowly

Frank DeGardini

Come, Thou Al- might - y King, Help us Thy name___ to sing, Help us to praise.
Fa-ther all glo - ri -ous, O'er all vic- to - ri - ous, Come and reign o - ver us, An- cient of days.

GOD OF OUR FATHERS

Text: Daniel Roberts

Music by
George W. Warren

Moderately
God of our fa - thers, whose al - might-y
hand Leads forth in beau - ty all the star-ry band
Of shin - ing worlds in splen-dor thru the skies,
Our grate - ful songs be - fore Thy throne a - rise.

A MIGHTY FORTRESS IS OUR GOD

Moderately
Martin Luther
A might-y fort-ress is our God, A
bul-wark nev-er fail - ing. Our help-er He a-
mid the flood of mor-tal ills pre-vail - ing, For
still our an-cient foe doth seek to work us
woe, His craft and pow'r are great, And

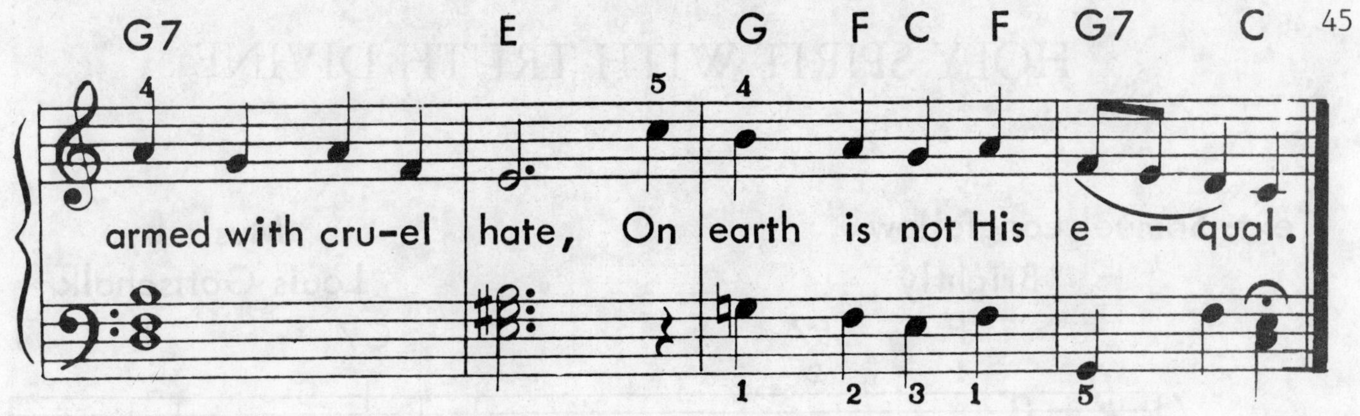
G7   E   G   F   C   F   G7   C
armed with cru-el hate, On earth is not His e - qual.

THE KING OF LOVE

Text: Herbert Baker

Music by
John B. Dykes

Rather fast

D   G   C   D   Em   D
mf The King of love my Shep-herd is, Whose
D7   G   D7   C   D
good-ness fail-eth nev-er, I noth-ing lack if
B7   Em   D7   C   D7   G D7   G
I am ___ His and He is mine for-ev - er.

HOLY SPIRIT WITH TRUTH DIVINE

Text: Samuel Longfellow
Brightly

Music by
Louis Gottschalk

Ho - ly spi - rit with truth di - vine,
Dawn up - on___ this heart of ___ mine.
Chase the shad - ows of night a - way,
Turn___ my dark - ness in - to day.

ALL HAIL THE POWER

Text: Edward Perronet
Slowly

Music by
Oliver Holden

All hail the power of Je - sus' name! Let
an - gels pros - trate fall. Bring forth the roy - al
di - a - dem, And crown Him Lord of ___
all! Bring forth the roy - al di - a - dem and
crown Him Lord ___ of all.

IN THE CROSS OF CHRIST

Text: John Bowring
Music by Ithamar Conkey
Moderately
In the cross of Christ I
When the woes of life o'er-
glo - ry, Tow - 'ring o'er the wrecks of
take me, Hopes de - ceive and fears an -
time. All the light of sa - cred
noy, Nev - er shall the cross for -
sto - ry Gath - ers 'round its head sub - lime.
sake me, Lo! It glows with peace and joy. A - men.

O JESUS, THOU ART STANDING

Text: William How

Music by
Justin Knecht

Allegretto

O Je-sus, ___ Thou art stand-ing, Out-
side the ___ fast-closed door, In low-ly ___ pa-tience
wait - ing to pass the ___ thresh - old o'er. We
bear the name of Chris-tians, His name and sign we ___ bear. O
shame, thrice shame up- on us, To keep Him standing there.

O WORSHIP THE KING

Text: Robert Grant
Music by
Michael Haydn
Moderately
p
O wor-ship the King, all glo-rious a-bove, O grate-ful-ly sing His pow-er and His love. Our shield and de-fend-er, the an-cient of days, Pa-vil-ioned in splen-dor and gird-ed with praise
O tell of His might, O sing of His grace. His robe is the light, His can-o-py space. His mer--cies how ten-der, how firm to the end, Our mak-er, de-fend-er, re-deem-er and friend!
mf
G D7 G D7 G D7 G D7 G D7 G D C D G D7 G D9 G D7 G D7 G D G

JESUS, SAVIOUR, PILOT ME

Text: Edward Hopper

Music by
John Gould

Slowly
Je-sus, Sav-iour, pi-lot me, O-ver
mf When at last I near the shore, And the
life's tem-pes-tuous sea. Un-known waves be-fore me
fear-ful break-ers roar, 'Twixt me and the peace-ful
roll, Hid-ing rock and treach'rous shoal. Chart and
rest, Then while lean-ing on Thy breast, May I
com-pass came from Thee. Je-sus, Sa-viour, pi-lot me!
hear Thee say to me, "Fear not, I will pi-lot thee."

BATTLE HYMN OF THE REPUBLIC

Text: Julia Ward Howe

Music by
William Steffe

With spirit
mf Mine eyes have seen the glo - ry of the
com-ing of the Lord, He is tramp-ling out the vin-tage where the
grapes of wrath are stored, He hath loosed the fate-ful light-ning of His
ter - ri - ble swift sword, His truth is march - ing on.
f Glo - ry! Glo - ry! Hal - le - lu - jah!

Glo-ry! Glo-ry! Hal-le-lu-jah! Glo-ry! Glo-ry! Hal-le-

lu-jah! His truth is march-ing on.

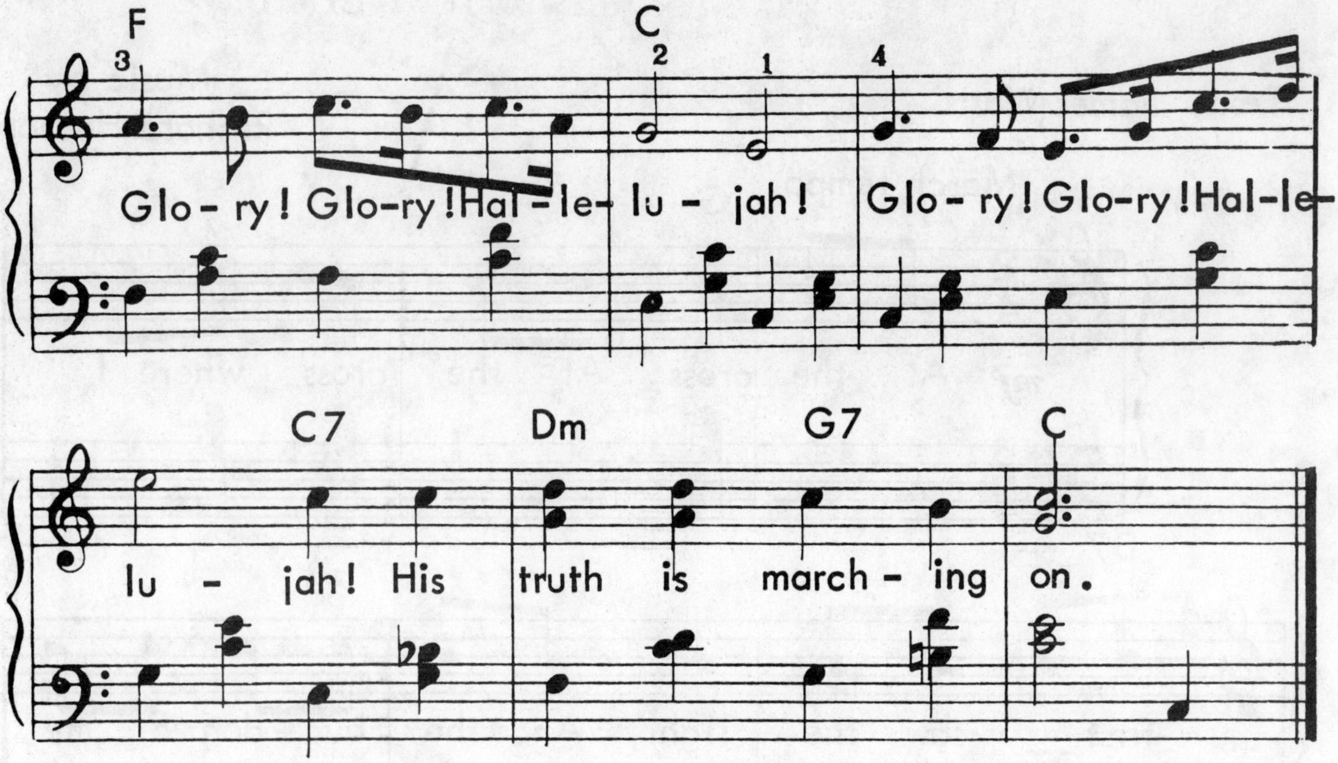

JUST AS I AM

Text: Charlotte Elliott

Music by
William Bradbury

Slowly

Just as I am, with-out one plea, But that Thy

blood was shed for me, And that Thou bidd'st me come to

Thee, O Lamb of God, I come, I come!

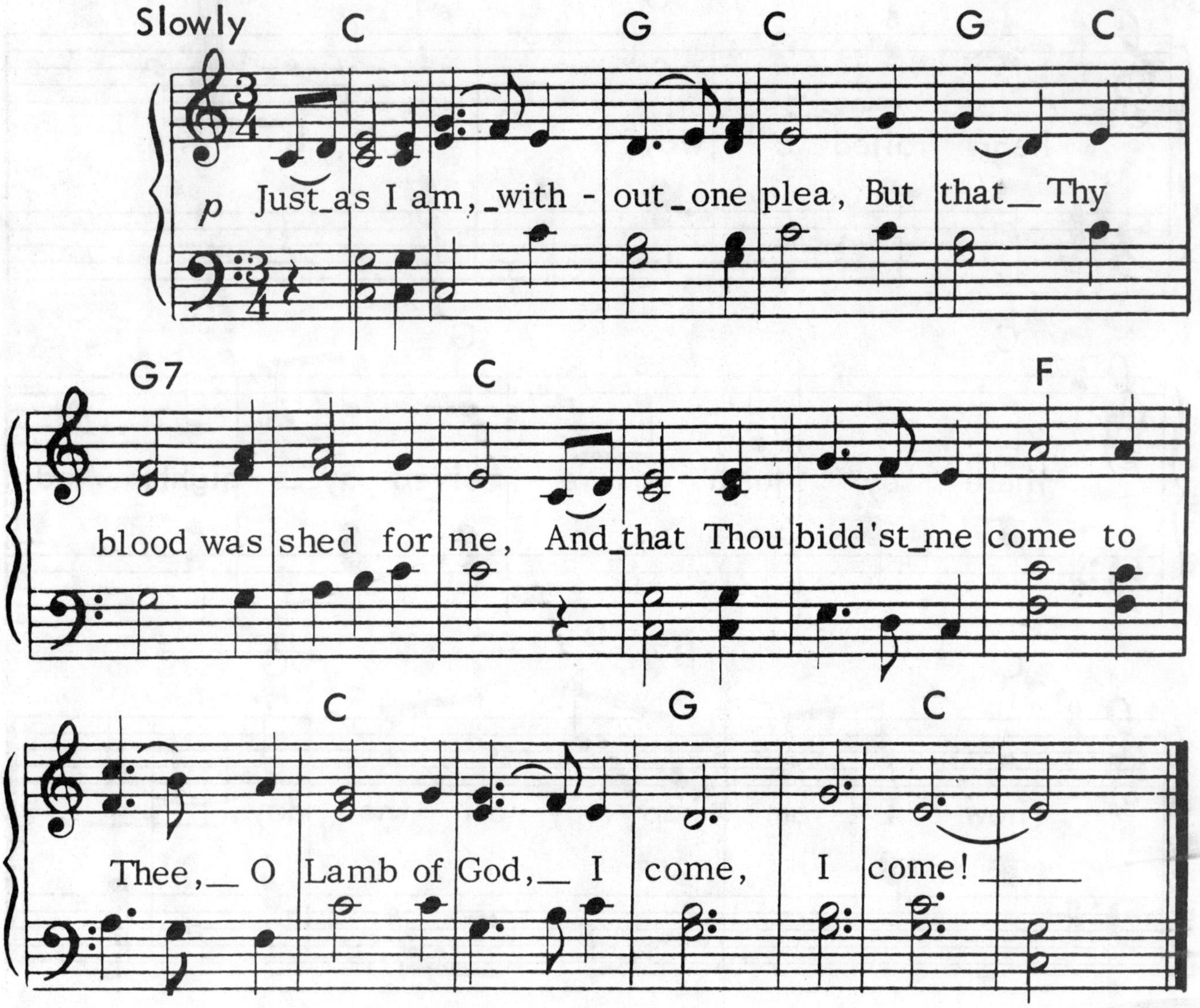

AT THE CROSS

Text: James Watts

Music by
Richard Hudson

March tempo
G
D7
G
C
G
C
D7
G
At the cross, At the cross where I
first saw the light, And the bur-den of my
heart rolled a-way, It was
there by faith I re-ceived my sight, And
now I am hap-py all the day.
mf

AMERICA

Text: Henry Carey

Traditional melody

Moderately
mf My coun - try, 'tis of thee, Sweet land of
li - ber - ty, Of thee I sing.
Land where my fa - thers died, Land of the
Pil - grims' pride, From ev ry
moun - tain side, Let free - dom ring.

HE LEADETH ME

Text: Joseph Gilmore

Music by
William Bradbury

Allegretto
He lead-eth me, O bless-ed thought! O
words with heav-en-ly com-fort fraught! Whate'er I do or
where I be, Still it's God's hand that lead-eth me.
CHORUS
He lead-eth me, He lead-eth me, By His own hand, He
lead-eth me. His faith-ful fol-low'r I would be, For

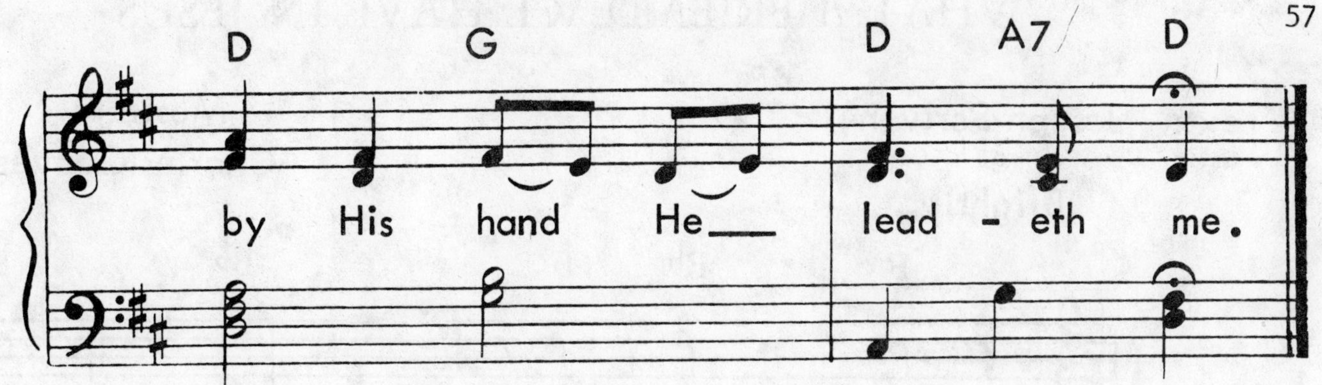
D   G   D   A7   D
by   His   hand   He___   lead - eth   me.

OUR FATHER IN HEAVEN

Slowly
C   F   C
p Our Fa - ther in Heav'n, we hal - low Thy name, May
F   C   G   C
Thy Kingdom ho - ly on earth be the same. O! give to us
G7   F   C
dai - ly our por - tion of bread, It
Dm G7 C Dm C G7   C
is from Thy boun - ty that all must___ be fed.

WHAT A FRIEND WE HAVE IN JESUS
58
Text: Joseph Scriven
Music by
Charles Converse
Brightly
mf
What a friend we have in Je - sus,
All our sins and grief to bear! What a pri - vi - lege to
car - ry Ev - 'ry-thing to God in prayer!
O what peace we of - ten for - feit,
O what need-less pain we bear, All be-cause we do not

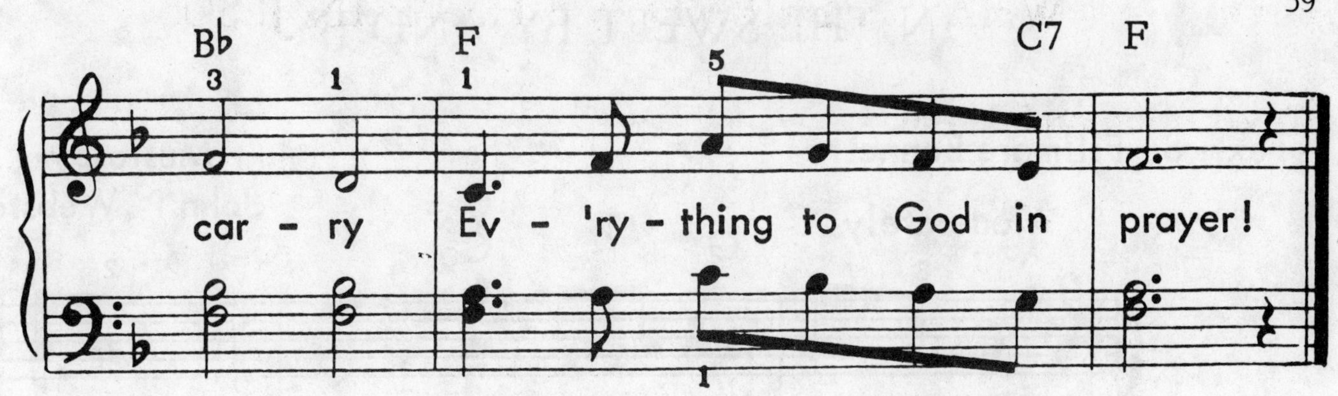

Bb
F
C7
F
car - ry
Ev - 'ry - thing to God in
prayer!

MY JESUS, I LOVE THEE

Gordon

Moderately
F
Bb
F
C7
p My
Je - sus, I
love__ Thee, I
know Thou art

F
Bb
C7
mine. For Thee all the
fol - lies of sin I re -

F
Bb
F
C7 F C
F
C7
sign. My gra - cious Re - deem - er, My
Sa - viour art

F
Bb
F
C7 F C7 F
Thou,__ If ev - er I
loved__ Thee, My Je - sus 'tis now.

IN THE SWEET BY AND BY

Text: S. Fillmore Bennett

Music by
John P. Webster

Moderately
mf There's a land that is fair-er than day, And by
faith we can see it a-far, For the Father waits over the
way, To pre-pare us a dwell-ing place there. In the
sweet by and by, We shall meet on that beauti-ful
shore. In the sweet by and

G
D7
G
by,
We shall
meet on that beau-ti-ful
shore.

SOFTLY NOW THE LIGHT OF DAY

Text: George Doane

Music: Carl M. Von Weber

Slowly   F   C7   Bb   F   E7   Am   C7
p
Soft - ly   now   the   light   of____   day,
F   Dm   A   F7   Bb   C   F
Fades   up - on   my   sight   a - way,
F   C7   Bb   F   E7   Am   C7
Free   from   care,   from   la - bor____   free,
F   F7   Bb   F   C7   F
Lord,   I   would__   com - mune   with   Thee.

GOD BE WITH YOU TILL WE MEET AGAIN

Text: Jeremiah Rankin

Music by
William Tomer

Moderately
mf God be with you till we meet a - gain!
By His coun-sels guide up-hold you, With His sheep securely
fold you, God be with you till we meet a-gain. Till we
meet,_ Till we meet, Till we meet at Je-sus_ feet, Till we
meet,_ Till we meet,_ God be with you till we meet a-gain.

MY TASK

Text: Maude Louise Ray

Music by
Edwin L. Ashford

Moderately
F   Bbm
To love some - one more dear - ly ev - 'ry
mf To fol - low truth as blind men long for
F   C7   F   E7   Am C
day,   To help a wand-'ring child to find the way,   To
light,   To do my best from dawn of day till night,   To
F   A7   D7
pon-der o'er a no - ble thought and pray,   And smile when
keep my heart fit for His ho - ly sight,   And an - swer
G7   C7   F7   Gm7 C7   F
eve-ning falls, And smile when eve-ning falls, This T is my task.
when He calls, And an-swer when He calls, This is my task.

ALL THROUGH THE NIGHT

Slowly
p Sleep, my child, and peace at - tend thee,
All thro' the night. Guard-ian an-gels God will send thee
All thro' the night. Soft the drow-sy hours are creeping
Hill and vale in slum-ber steep-ing, I my lov-ing
vi - gil keep-ing, All thro' the night.

FOR ALL THE SAINTS

Text: William W. How

Music by
R. Vaughan Williams

Brightly
mf For all the saints who from their la-bors rest, Who Thee by faith be-
fore the world con - fessed, Thy name, O Je - sus, be for-ev - er - blest, Al -
le - lu - ia! Al - le - lu - ia!

Slow, with feeling
p 1. If when you give the best of your
ser-vice, Tell-ing the world that the Sav-iour has
come, Be not dis-mayed when men don't be-
lieve you, He'll un-der-stand____ and
say____ "Well done."
CHORUS:
Oh, when I

Eb   Bb7
come   to the   end   of my   jour-ney,   Wea - ry of
Eb   Eb
life   and the   bat-tle is   won,   Car-r'ing the
Eb7   Ab   Eb
staff   and the   Cross   of re - demp-tion,
Ab   D   Eb   C   F7   Bb7   Eb
He'll   un - der - stand___ and   say___ "Well done.".

2nd Verse:
Misunderstood, the Saviour of sinners,
Hung on the cross, He was God's
    only Son,
Oh! Hear Him call His Father in
    heaven,
"Let not my will, but Thine, be done."

(Repeat Chorus)

3rd Verse:
If when this life of labor is
    ended,
And the reward of the race
    you have run,
Oh the sweet rest prepared
    for the faithful,
Will be His blest and final
    "Well Done." (Chorus)

JESUS LOVES ME

With spirit
mf
Je - sus loves me, This I know,
For the Bi - ble tells me so. Lit - tle ones to
Him be -long, They are weak but He is strong.
CHORUS:
f Yes, Je -sus loves me! Yes, Je -sus loves me!
Yes, Je -sus loves me! The Bi - ble tells me so.

CHRIST, THE LIFE OF ALL THE LIVING

Text: Ernst Homburg

Music: Traditional
(Darmstadt, Germany)

With spirit

Christ, the Life of all the liv-ing Christ, the Death of death, our foe,
Who, Thy-self for me once giv-ing To the darkest depths of woe,
Through Thy suf-f'ring, death and mer-it, I e-ter-nal life in-her-it,
Thou-sand thousand thanks shall be, Dear-est Je-sus, un-to Thee.

GO TELL IT ON THE MOUNTAIN

Moderate
G   G7
mf The shep-herds feared and trem-bled, When
Am7   G7
high a-bove the earth, Rang out an an-gel
A7   D7
cho-rus To hail our Sa-viour's birth.
CHORUS:
G   Am   G   Am7   D7
Go tell it on the moun-tain, O-ver the hills and
G   Am
ev-'ry-where. Go tell it on the

G
Am7
D7
G
moun - tain, Our Je - sus Christ___ is born!

GOD NOW IS WITH US

Text: Petrus Herbert

Music by
Friedrich F. Fleming

Slowly

G
D7
G
C
p
God now is with us, For the night is
G   D7   G
B7
Em
Am
clos - ing. The light and dark - ness are of His dis -
Em   B7   G
D7
G   A7
pos - ing, And 'neath His shad - ow here to rest we
D   A7   D
G   C
G   D7
G   C   G
yield___ us, For He will shield___ us, A - men.

EVENING PRAYER

Engelburt Humperdinck

Moderately
p When at night I go to sleep, Fourteen angels
watch do __ keep, Two my head are guard - ing,
Two my feet are guid - ing, Two are on my right hand,
Two are on my left hand __ and __ Two who warm - ly
cov - er, Two who o'er me hov - er, Two to whom 'tis
*Octave lower, ad lib

C Bb C Bb F C7 F7 Bb
giv - en To guide my steps to Heav - en.

NOW I LAY ME DOWN TO SLEEP

Moderately
C F C G7 C
Now I lay me down to sleep, I

F C G C G G+
pray the Lord my soul to keep, And

C F C E E7 F Fm
if I'm called be - fore I wake, I

C F C G7 C
pray the Lord my soul to take.

WERE YOU THERE?

SPIRITUAL
Slowly
Were you there when they cru - ci - fied my
Lord?
Were you there when they
nailed Him to the Cross?
Oh!
Some-times it
caus - es me to trem-ble, trem-ble, trem-ble, Were you

F   F7   Bb   C   F
there when they laid Him in the tomb?

O LOVE THAT WILL NOT LET ME GO

Text by George Matheson

Music by
Albert L. Peace

Moderate

G   D7
mf O Love that will not let me go __ I

G   B7
rest my wea - ry soul in Thee, __ I give Thee back the life I

Em   A7
owe, __ That in Thine o - cean depths its

G   D7 G   C   G
flow, May rich - er, full - er be. A - men.

THE LITTLE BROWN CHURCH IN THE VALE

Brightly
William S. Pitts
Bb
F
mf There's a church in the vale by the wild-wood, No
F7 Bb Eb
love-li - er place in the dale. No_ spot is so dear to my
Bb F7 Bb
child - hood, As the lit - tle brown church in the vale, O_
p come come come come Come to the church in the wild-wood, O
mf
F Bb Eb
come to the church in the dale! No_ spot is so dear to my

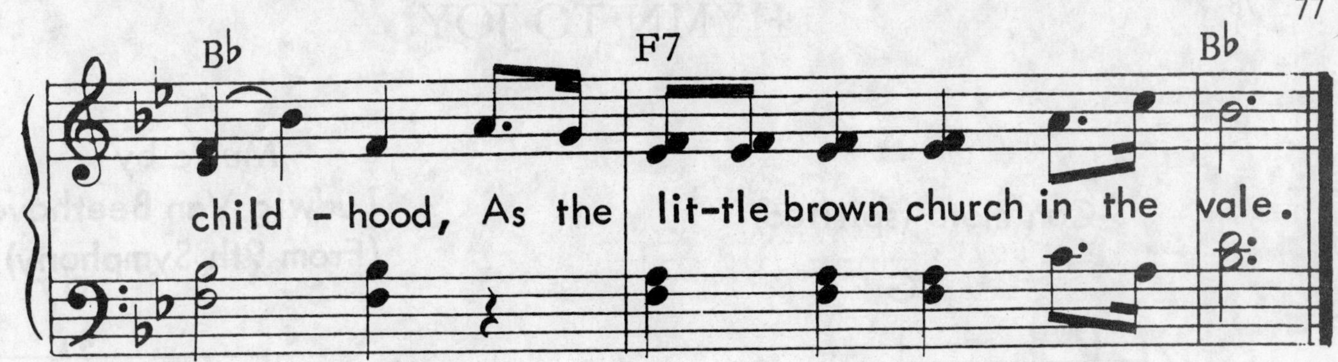
Bb
F7
Bb
child - hood, As the lit-tle brown church in the vale.

OUR GOD, OUR HELP

Text: Isaac Watts
Moderately

Music by
William Croft

C
Am F G C
mp Our God, our help in ag - es past, Our

Am D7 Em
C F G
Hope for years to come! Our Shel - ter from the

C C° G
F C G7 C
storm - y blast, And our E - ter - nal Home!

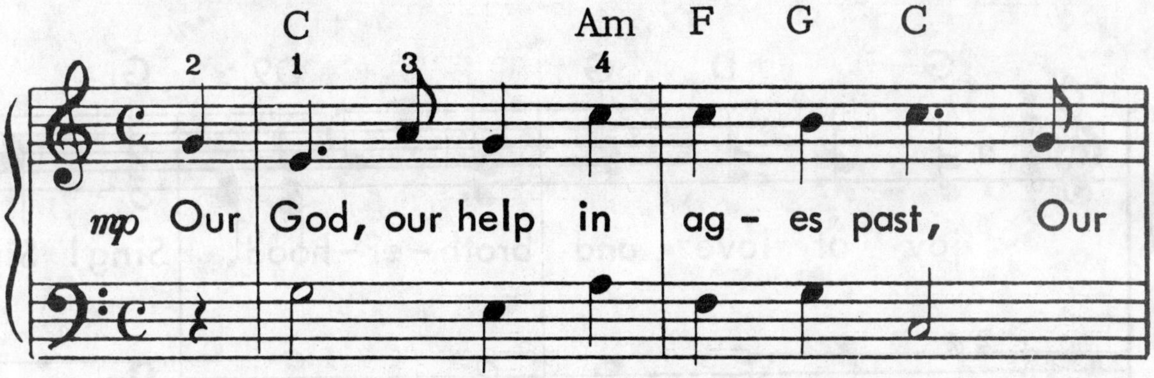

HYMN TO JOY

Con moto (spirited)
Music by
Ludwig Van Beethoven
(From 9th Symphony)
mf Sing! Sing a Hymn To Joy, The
joy of love and broth-er-hood. Sing! Sing a
Hymn To Joy, The joy of peace when life is good.
Joy comes in love and in play and

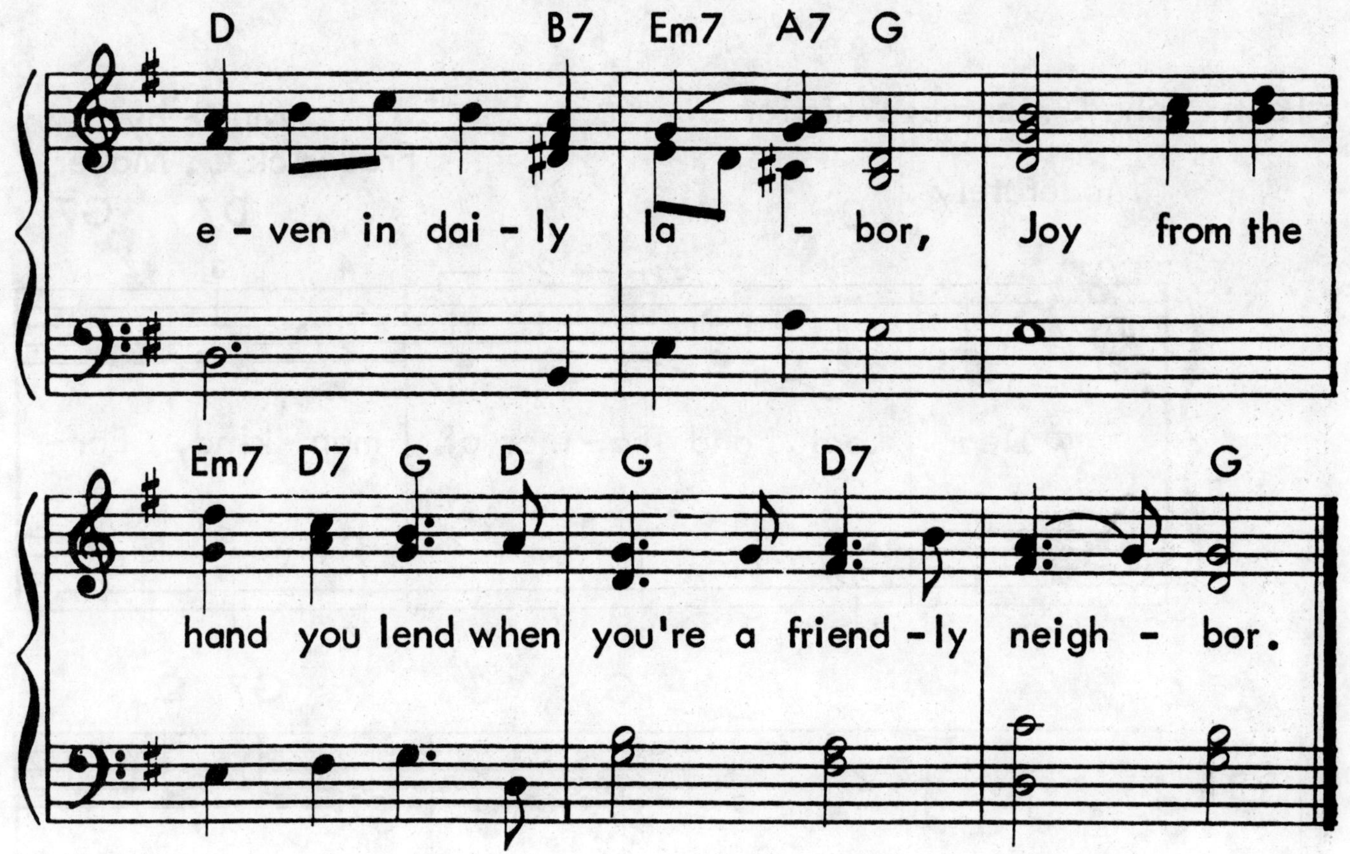

D   B7 Em7 A7 G
e - ven in dai - ly la - bor, Joy from the
Em7 D7 G D G D7 G
hand you lend when you're a friend -ly neigh - bor.

2nd time:

Sing! Sing a Hymn To Joy,

In ev'ry heart may joy abound.

Make the hymn a song of joy,

From pole to pole the world around.

Life can be beautiful when the value of love
   is understood,

Sing! Sing a Hymn To Joy —

To Peace, to Love, to Brotherhood!

DEAR LORD AND FATHER OF MANKIND

Text: John Greenleaf Whittier

Music by
Frederick C. Maker

Moderately
C
D7   G7
mp Dear Lord and Fa-ther of man-kind, For-
C   G   C   G7 C
give our fe-ver-ish ways. Re-clothe us in our
E7   G   F   A7   Dm   D
right-ful mind, In pur-er lives Thy
G7   C C7   Bb F   Fo   C   F C
ser-vice find, In deep-er rev-'rence praise. Amen

MY ONE LAST HOPE

Text: Latouche Hancock
Moderately

Music by
Louis Gottschalk

My hope, my one___ last hope is
Thee! Though tired with sor - row, I on - ly
see That Thou a - lone___ doth
pit - y me, My___ one___ last
hope ___ is Thee, is Thee!

BEAUTIFUL ISLE OF SOMEWHERE

Words: Jessie Pounds

Music: John S. Fearis

Verse
Slowly
G
Am7   D7
1. Some-where the sun is shin - ing,
Some-where the song - birds dwell.
G
Hush then thy sad re - pin - ing.
G°   D   C°
A7   G   A7   D
God lives and all is well.
CHORUS
D7   G
Some - where, Some - where,

Em G A7 D7 Fo Am7 D7
Beau - ti - ful Isle___ of Some - where.
G C G D G C Cm
Land of the true, Where we live a - new -
G D7 G
Beau - ti - ful Isle___ of Some - where.
2 3 4 5

2. Somewhere the day is longer,
   Somewhere the task is done.
   Somewhere the heart is stronger,
   Somewhere new hopes are begun.

   (CHORUS)

3. Somewhere the load is lifted,
   Somewhere there's Heaven's gate.
   Somewhere the clouds are rifted,
   Somewhere the angels wait.

   (CHORUS)

LET US BREAK BREAD TOGETHER

Moderately slow
mf
Let us break bread to - geth - er on our
knees, _____ Let us break bread to - geth-er on our
knees. _____ When I fall on my knees with my
face to the ris - ing sun, Oh Lord! Have

Gm   C7   F   Gm   F
mer - cy   on   me.   Let   us   praise   God   to-
Bb   F   C7   F   Dm
geth - er   on   our   knees, —— Let   us   praise   God   to-
G7   C   Bb   Dm   F   Cm
geth - er   on   our   knees, —— Oh! When   I   fall   on   my
D7   Gm   Bbm   C7
knees   with   my   face   to   the   ris - ing   sun,   Oh! ___
F   Bb   C7   F
Lord!   Have   mer - cy   if ___ you   please. ___

THE GREAT SPECKLED BIRD

Traditional

Moderately
C   C7   F
mp What a beau-ti-ful thought I am think-ing,
G7
Con - cern - ing the Great Speckled Bird.
C
C7   F
Re - mem-ber her name is re - cord - ed
G7
On the pag - es of pure shin-ing gold.
C

2. All the other birds flock all around her,
   But she is despised by the squad.
   Oh the Great Speckled Bird in the bible
   Is the one with the great church of God.

3. When He cometh descending from Heaven,
   On the cloud, as He wrote in His word,
   I'll be joyfully carried up to meet Him —
   On the wings of the Great Speckled Bird.

SILENT NIGHT

Text: Josef Mohr

Music by
Franz Gruber

Calmly
C
p Si - lent night! Ho - ly night!
G7   C   F
All is calm, all is bright. 'Round yon
C   F
vir - gin Moth-er and Child, Ho - ly In-fant so
C   G°   Dm   G7   C
ten - der and mild, Sleep in heav-en-ly peace,
G7   C
Sleep in heav - en - ly peace.

WHISPERING HOPE

Moderately
Alice Hawthorne
p Soft as the voice of an an - gel, Breath-ing a
les - son un - heard, Hope, with a gen-tle per-
sua - sion, Whis-pers her com-fort-ing word.
Wait till the dark-ness is o - ver,
Wait till the tem-pest is done, Hope for the

G7   C   C
sun-shine to-mor - row,   Af - ter the
G7   C   Refrain: G7
show - er is gone.   mf   Whis - per-ing
C   G7
hope, __ Oh how wel - come thy
C   F   C°
voice, __ Mak - ing my
C   G7   C
heart __ in its sor - row re - joice. __

Brightly
mf Now sing we, now re - joice, ___ Now
raise to heav'n our voice. __ He from whom joy
stream - eth, poor in a man-ger lies. __ Not so bright-ly
beam - eth the sun in yon - der skies. ___
Thou my Sa - viour art! _____ Thou my Sa-viour art!

JOY TO THE WORLD

Text: Isaac Watts

Music by
George Friedrich Handel

With spirit

Joy to the world! The Lord is come, Let
earth re- ceive her King, Let ev - 'ry __ heart pre-
pare __ Him __ room, __ And heav'n and na - ture __
sing, And __ heav'n and na - ture __ sing, And __
heav'n, and heav'n __ and __ na - ture sing.

WHEN THE SAINTS GO MARCHING IN

Moderately
SPIRITUAL
mf
I am just a lone - ly trav-'ler,
Thro' this big wide world of sin,
Want to join that grand pro - ces - sion,
When the Saints go march - ing in.

CHORUS
F   C7   F   C7   F
mf
Oh when the Saints go march-ing in,
C7   F   Dm7   F   C7
Oh when the Saints go march-ing in,
F   F7   Bb
Lord, I want to be in that num-ber,
Fo   F   G7   C7   F   Bb   F
When the Saints go march-ing in.

HE'S GOT THE WHOLE WORLD IN HIS HANDS

Steady moderate beat

SPIRITUAL

He's got the whole world in His hands,
He's got the whole wide world in His hands,
He's got the whole world in His hands,
He's got the whole world in His hands.
*(1) He's got the earth and sky, in His hands,

C7
He's got the night and day___ in His hands, ___
F
F6
He's got the sun and moon ____
F
F6
C7
1-2
in His hands, ____ He's got the whole world
F
3 C7
in His hands. He's got the whole world
F
in His hands.

* 2nd time: Land and sea, wind and rain, spring and fall.
3rd time: Young and old, rich and poor, Yes He's got ev'ryone
in His hands.

CHRIST, THE LORD, IS RISEN TO-DAY

Slowly

Lyra Davidica

Christ, the Lord, is ris'n to - day, ____
Al - le - lu - ia! Sons of men and angels say ____
Al - le - lu - ia! Raise your joys and tri-umphs high
Al - le - lu - ia! Sing, __ ye __ heav'ns and
earth re - ply, Al - le - lu - ia!